DEVIL LAND

Desi Moreno-Penson

BROADWAY PLAY PUBLISHING INC
New York
www.broadwayplaypublishing.com
info@broadwayplaypublishing.com

DEVIL LAND
© Copyright 2011 by Desi Moreno-Penson

Cover photo by Ryan Kravetz
First printing: November 2011
I S B N: 978-0-88145-514-4
Book design: Marie Donovan
Page make-up: Adobe Indesign
Typeface: Palatino
Printed and bound in the U S A

DEVIL LAND was first produced as part of the 4th Annual Summer Play Festival (Founder/Executive Producer: Arielle Tepper Madover; Managing Director: Erika Feldman) in the Lion Theater at the 42nd Street Times Square Theater Center in New York City from 31 July thru 5 August 2007. The cast and creative contributors were:

AMERICO ....Bryant Mason
BEATRIZ .... Vanessa Aspillaga
DESTINY...Jenny Seastone Stern
THE VOICE OF THE NARRATOR........................D J Thacker

Director..Jose Zayas
Stage manager...Wesley Apfel
Set designer...Ryan Kravetz
Sound designer...David M Lawson.

CHARACTERS & SETTING

AMERICO, *early 30s-to-late 40s, building superintendent, easy to anger, overbearing, highly insecure, guilt-ridden, a pedophile...can mimic the Dr Seuss character, the Grinch, from* How the Grinch Stole Christmas.

BEATRIZ, *early 30s–mid 40s, Super's wife, sexually repressed, religious fanatic, mentally unstable, can be maternal, but capable of being fiercely and viciously combative.*

DESTINY, *this character is 12 years old. Will be played by an adult actress. Emotionally complex character with an especially vivid imagination.*

THE VOICE OF THE NARRATOR; *we never actually 'see' this character —we can only hear him, but his voice should remind us of Boris Karloff's from the old television program,* How the Grinch Stole Christmas.

Time and Place: The present. A boiler room. The kind of boiler room that can be found in any Bronx apartment building. It's important to remember, however that this room shall "change", —by the end of the play, it should look less like a boiler room and more like a room that has been occupied by some mystical and bizarre supernatural force.

ACT ONE

(Scene: We see the strangely lit confines of a boiler room. There are pipes everywhere; the walls are black with soot. Oil slicks can be seen all over the floor. There are windows, but in this oppressively dark space, they are bricked over or covered with plywood. The boiler is located stage right. To the left, there is a dirt-stained, yellowish vinyl curtain that lines the side of a small "living" area of the stage. We see a small cot with a pillow. We also see an icebox, a working fan, and a child's bookcase with no books, a small kitchenette set that has a few chairs missing, a covered bucket, and a selection of children's cereal boxes, Lucky Charms, Apple Jacks, and Cap'n Crunch, etc.)

(Lights on BEATRIZ.*)*

BEATRIZ: I hate the rain.

My grandmother used to say that it rains more in the Bronx

Because the Bronx is more sinful than any other place in New York.

And that makes God cry.

The water is not pure. It's not.

If you're ever in the Bronx, and it's raining… Stick your tongue out, and taste it.

Taste the water.

You'll see what I'm talking about.

This is not *pure water*…!

Like a blessing. Like tears from Heaven.
It's *filthy*. And evil.
And evil's got to go somewhere, right?
So it seeps in through the cracks of the apartment
buildings
It settles into the grass, choking the jade from the lawns
It percolates out into the air, sharpening everything
that we breathe
Like a knife slicing into our lungs—
Especially on a cold day
A cold and stormy day in the sinful Bronx.

(AMERICO *enters. He is dressed in the typical working-clothes of an apartment building superintendent; complete with institutional green pants and tool belt.*)

AMERICO: *¿Nadie te vio, verdad?*

BEATRIZ: No. Nobody saw me.

AMERICO: Have you checked the windows?

BEATRIZ: No. No I haven't checked them. Is there any light coming through?

AMERICO: No. There's no light.

(*A frozen moment between* AMERICO *and* BEATRIZ.)

AMERICO: There's no light. And the streets are wet again. We have to take the trashcans out back tonight.

BEATRIZ: I won't touch the cans.

AMERICO: Those kids will open the hydrant. If I leave the trashcans out there, in the morning, all the garbage will be wet and it'll smell like death outside our door.

BEATRIZ: It smells like death now.

AMERICO: Her mother lives in our building…!

BEATRIZ: I know—

AMERICO: You took a kid whose mother lives in our building. She's on the third floor.

BEATRIZ: *(Nodding)* Apartment 3B.

AMERICO: Why did you do this? Why? This is kidnapping. You know that? And it's kidnapping in our own backyard...it's not like you took some kid from Brooklyn or Staten Island.

BEATRIZ: I don't know anybody in Brooklyn and I've never been to Staten Island.

AMERICO: And you didn't even take a really, little kid...you know, like somebody who's fice or six years old? A small kid.

BEATRIZ: It just seemed right. She was there. It was easy.

AMERICO: She's too fucking big!

BEATRIZ: Keep your voice down. *(A beat)* I told her to come to our apartment. "It's going to be all right, honey...," I told her, "...It's going to be fine. Your mommy will understand." She called me from the candy store across the street and she wanted me to find her mother so she could get more money to buy a notebook for school. "Come over to our apartment," I said. I told her I'd call her mother. I even said I'd lend her the money for the notebook. When she got to our place she was smiling. She was so easy to talk to. I noticed that about her. And she believed every word I told her. Every single word I said. That's how I knew I had to give her a lot of attention. She was hungry for it.

AMERICO: But just because she came to you didn't mean you had to take her.

BEATRIZ: She watched me the whole time...

AMERICO: What do we do when the cops start coming around? What if they want to search the whole building?

BEATRIZ: *(Lost in her thoughts)* She watched me the whole time I pretended to talk to her mother on the phone—

AMERICO: Are you fucking listening to me? We know this kid. Bea, she knows us. Don't you understand? *(Silence)* We have to give her back to her mother. It's going to be okay. We'll fix this. We'll give her back to her moms. And then we'll go away. We'll go far away. Maybe we'll go to Puerto Rico.

BEATRIZ: No. We can't do that.

AMERICO: Fuck it, we'll go.

BEATRIZ: No!

AMERICO: Yes! We'll move there, and I'll get a job. We'll start over.

BEATRIZ: I won't go. They'll hate us there.

AMERICO: Bea—we got family in P R; they'll let us stay with them for awhile until we can get settled.

BEATRIZ: I won't go! They'll hate us 'cause we're gringos…!

AMERICO: We're not gringos…somos Boricuas…!

BEATRIZ: We're Ricans who were born here, and we never learned how to speak Spanish.

AMERICO: I can speak Spanish.

BEATRIZ: Sometimes when you speak Spanish, you sound like a white person trying to speak Spanish.

AMERICO: Fuck you…I speak good.

BEATRIZ: I won't go…

AMERICO: Better to go to P R, than go to jail….

(Again, sullen silence from BEATRIZ)

AMERICO: How…How do we do this? I'm the Super.
I've got work to do in this damn building all the time.
All the time…! You know this. We'll have to come
down here…constantly… To check on her…to feed
her…to wash her… You didn't think about any of that,
did you?

BEATRIZ: I'll do it. You just concentrate on your work.

AMERICO: Bullshit.

BEATRIZ: *(She becomes busy with activities, starts preparing
the room)* No. Really. I'll take care of her. I already love
her. You have to learn to love her. Men learn to love.
It doesn't come natural. With women, it's more natural.

AMERICO: There's no bathroom in here, how will she
do her business?

BEATRIZ: *(Showing him)* This bucket. It's pretty big.

AMERICO: Jesus… It's going to smell in here.

BEATRIZ: We'll keep it covered with a pot lid. We're the
only ones who come down, so we don't have to worry
about anybody else smelling it.

AMERICO: Do we take turns cleaning it out?

BEATRIZ: I'll do it. I'll do all of it. I'm going to be a good
mother.

AMERICO: *(Laughs)* Cleaning up piss and shit don't
make you a good mother.

BEATRIZ: *(Slight petulance)* I know that.

AMERICO: *(A beat)* Is she asleep?

BEATRIZ: Yes.

AMERICO: Did you use something?

BEATRIZ: Yes. The pills the doctor gave me.

AMERICO: *(Concerned)* But that's what you use. *(A beat)* Will she sleep long?

BEATRIZ: Yes.

AMERICO: For how long?

BEATRIZ: I don't know.

AMERICO: What do we tell her when she wakes up?

BEATRIZ: That we're a family.

(Blackout on AMERICO *and* BEATRIZ. *Lights up only on* AMERICO. *He addresses the audience.)*

AMERICO: *(Making the sign of the cross)* Bless me Father, for I have sinned
It's been five months since my last confession.
Father, I married a woman I can never make happy.
I don't know if that's a sin or not
But it feels like it.
I can't make her happy 'cause I can't love God the way she does.
I'm not saying I don't love God, Father.
I love Him a lot. Jesus is good people.
But I don't think about him all the time, you know?
Not like her, not like my wife.
She lives for God, the way plants live for water. And air.
It was her Abuela that got her thinking like that.
Man, her Abuela HATED me. She wanted Beatriz to become a nun.
(Laughs) But I got to her first; you know what I'm saying?
Beatriz said she liked me because I had a job
And I didn't make fun of God.
And when I told her I hadn't slept with a lot of women
She said that made me purer and cleaner than most men.

She said she'd be proud to be the wife of a man
Who didn't need to be with every girl in the
neighborhood,
That's good, right?
(A beat) But that don't mean I don't like sex!
Look, Father—I respect my wife, okay? I like the way
she carries herself.
Like a queen.
So righteous and regal.
A queen for God.
I respect her for not being like the other girls around
here.
Especially the young ones…the ones without
husbands…I see them…coming in all hours of the
night…leaving their kids with girlfriends, while they're
out having sex with God knows how many men…
always with the high heels y los pantalones apretados
showing the thong panties in the back—
I can't be with a woman like that, Father.
Those women are disgusting.
But Father, I got to live, right?

(Blackout. Lights up on DESTINY. *She awakens, then
suddenly sits up, alert. We hear the* NARRATOR'S VOICE.*)*

NARRATOR'S VOICE: Once there was a girl named
Destiny
Who woke up and she opened her eyes
Only to see she'd been stolen like Christmas
And it was all a very nasty surprise.

*(Outside, we hear the fading sounds of the Mr Softee ice
cream truck. This comforts* DESTINY *somewhat. She looks
around, taking in the room.)*

NARRATOR'S VOICE: She listened to the Mr Softee
melody
It calmed her down a bit

The thought of ice cream
Brought a smile to her face
And she'd love a banana split!
But then she remembered the strange lady who took
her
And brought her down to this gloomy place

(BEATRIZ *enters. Playwright's note: The following passages
can either be staged as a mime or a non-verbal tableau
between* BEATRIZ *and* DESTINY. *The important thing to
remember is that we should only hear the* NARRATOR *at this
point.*)

NARRATOR'S VOICE: "We're a family now…" The
woman had said.
"A family?" Destiny pondered this with a puzzled face.
It was a funny bit of news
For the child to take in
For Destiny had her own mommy
Thank you very much
And besides, wasn't switching mommies
Something like a 'sin'?
"It's only a sin if you're not grateful,"
The strange woman told her, "All grateful children are
given a hand."
But then she leaned in to whisper, "It's only the
unbaptized, you see,
The lesser ones…
The liars—
Those children have to go to Devil Land."
"Devil Land?" Destiny asked.
"Yes, Devil Land," The woman replied.
"Devil Land's a room…an alcove of doom.
There, bad children will weep
And never again, shall they sleep
They cry, and they squeal, and they'll always try to flee

They're desperate, and panic-stricken,
So frantic for their liberty
But it isn't the "Big Hell".
It's not the room with brimstone and fire.
My grandmother told me all about Devil Land,
And she was certainly no liar."

(BEATRIZ *moves to another place on stage.* AMERICO
enters.)

NARRATOR'S VOICE: And as time passed
Destiny tried to stay meekly in her place
She saw the odd man go about his business with the
boiler
Always with his gruffly stern face.
She hated the din and dark of that room.
She marveled at its singular lack of light and air.

DESTINY: They shut up the sun.

I know they did.
Even though, I know it's still out there...somewhere.
There's no light to read.
I wanted to read so I could forget the heat.
In here, it's not good heat.

NARRATOR'S VOICE: Destiny spent all her time talking
With her imaginary friend, the Grinch
He'd always been true enough for her
And was as real as a spiteful pinch.

DESTINY: Remember that time mommy took us to
Puerto Rico...?
That's good heat. The heat there loves me.
Because it comes straight from the Sun.
Not from pipes.
Not like here.
Warmth don't come out of metal.

NARRATOR'S VOICE: She tried to escape once

And was quickly dragged back
That's when they brought the chain in
To keep her down

(BEATRIZ *holds a struggling* DESTINY *down upon the cot as* AMERICO *brings out a long, heavy chain, and attaches it to* DESTINY's *leg.*)

NARRATOR'S VOICE: And for the first time ever,
The strange woman was unhappy with Destiny
She regarded the child with an angry frown,
She accused her of being hateful,
She warned her once again of Devil Land, and declared…

BEATRIZ: Destiny, you're not being grateful.

DESTINY: *(Tearful)* I'm sorry, I'm sorry…I'm just *so scared*!

NARRATOR'S VOICE: Poor Destiny
Talking to her friend, the Grinch, evermore
He was angry because the strange lady
Had lured her from that candy store
Destiny didn't take his counsel then
And she promised she'd do better.
She'd listen to his advice
Right down to the letter
Perhaps they could come up with a plan, together?
Something safe…
Something secure…
Nothing too risky, or even quixotic—

DESTINY: Wait a minute! Wait a minute!

NARRATOR'S VOICE: Destiny cried—

DESTINY: Wait a minute. I think I've got it!
What about the boiler?
Maybe you could hide in the boiler, while they're here.

Oh yes!

If you're in the boiler

And if they're mean to me, I'll tell them you're in there

Getting hot. Getting mad.

That'll scare them, huh?

I'll make it sound really scary and you can help me.

(Blackout. Lights up. BEATRIZ *is now seated at the kitchenette table along with* DESTINY. *She is noticeably nervous.* AMERICO *is adjusting and fiddling with a chain attached to a pipe and is fixing a shackle around* DESTINY's *ankle.)*

BEATRIZ: *(To* AMERICO; *irritated)* Aren't you finished yet?

AMERICO: Just give me a second.

BEATRIZ: You've been there for an hour.

AMERICO: Will you relax?

BEATRIZ: She hasn't eaten today, and the soup is getting cold.

AMERICO: Then go ahead and *eat…*! God…what the fuck is wrong with you?

BEATRIZ: No, don't do that. Don't use God and fuck in the same sentence.

DESTINY: I'm not hungry.

BEATRIZ: *(Brightly to her)* It doesn't matter, honey. You have to eat something. *(To* AMERICO; *irritated)* The tenants will hear that noise—

AMERICO: So what?

DESTINY: They'll think it's a ghost.

AMERICO: Yeah, there you go…!

BEATRIZ: I didn't say that.

DESTINY: But they will. The people…when they hear the chain rattling… they'll think it's a ghost. And they'll say the building's on top of an Indian burial ground. I saw that in a movie.

AMERICO: Indian ghosts in the Bronx? *(Laughs)*

BEATRIZ: Don't laugh at her.

DESTINY: Uh-huh…we're Indians, right? Mami says we all come from Caribbean Indians in Puerto Rico.

BEATRIZ: That's a different kind of Indian.

DESTINY: And those Indians are called Tainos.

BEATRIZ: But we're not Tainos anymore, honey—

AMERICO: *(With one final tug on the chain)* Okay, this should hold.

BEATRIZ: We're civilized people now.

DESTINY: *(Seeing the soup tureen and bowls)* Are we going to eat?

BEATRIZ: Yes, we're all going to sit down and eat. Together.

DESTINY: It's too hot in here to eat.

BEATRIZ: *(Serving her)* I know. But you need to eat something. Come sit down.

DESTINY: I can't. It's too hot.

BEATRIZ: Try. I want you to try.

DESTINY: I can't.

BEATRIZ: You can.

AMERICO: Don't force her.

BEATRIZ: I'm not going to let her starve herself in front of me. *(A pause)* Bless us, Oh Lord, for these, thy gifts, that we are about to receive from thy bounty. Amen.

AMERICO: Hallelujah! *(To* DESTINY*)* Destiny, would you like to live in Puerto Rico?

BEATRIZ: Americo…!

AMERICO: *(Still to* DESTINY*)* Because I know how you feel. It's too fucking hot, it's smelly, you can hear the mice scratching behind the walls, car alarms going off every five minutes, even if you're just looking at the damn car, the boiler never stops rumbling, and the windows here are always covered so you never know if it's night or day. But Puerto Rico…! Aaah…Puerto Rico is gleaming and warm…Puerto Rico is cool waters you can swim in, and smooth palm leaves you can touch. Puerto Rico is the Motherland…

BEATRIZ: That's enough…

AMERICO: No. I think I'm on to something here. I want to be a Taino Indian, too. I want to walk naked on a beach with a nose ring and long strands of gold hanging down low from my ears…

*(*DESTINY *giggles.)*

AMERICO: *(Grins)* Look Bea—I made her laugh. *(To* DESTINY*)* You like that, huh?

BEATRIZ: No one is going to live naked on a beach. Eat your soup.

DESTINY: If I eat some soup, can I go upstairs and see my mommy?

BEATRIZ: No.

AMERICO: *(To* BEATRIZ*; worriedly)* Bea—

BEATRIZ: *(Coldly)* Your mommy's not here anyway. She left the building a few days ago and she hasn't come back.

(An uncomfortable beat)

DESTINY: Is she looking for me?

BEATRIZ: I don't know. Maybe she moved away.

AMERICO: No. Don't say that to her. Her mother loves her. *(To* DESTINY*)* Your mother loves you, Destiny. She'll come back for you.

BEATRIZ: *(To him; furiously)* How do you know that?

AMERICO: Because she's her mother.

BEATRIZ: My mother left me and never came back. She left me with my grandmother, and SHE was the one who raised me.

AMERICO: That's different. Your mother died. Destiny's mother is still alive.

BEATRIZ: People can leave and not come back. It can happen.

AMERICO: I know it can happen. I'm just saying that's not what happened to Destiny's mother.

BEATRIZ: You don't know that! Things happen. And when they do, nobody cares. Destiny's mother lives like a cat in heat. She doesn't even go to church.

AMERICO: What has that got to do with anything?

BEATRIZ: If someone doesn't go to church it means they don't fear God. And if you don't fear God, then you live in a world without gravity, and one strong wind will be enough to knock your body right off the planet and nobody will care—

AMERICO: Bea—come on.

BEATRIZ: Look how easy it was for us to take her. Her mother wasn't around. And neither was anybody else. Because nobody cares. *(To* DESTINY; *intensely)* You're Puerto Rican. You're a Puerto Rican girl and you're in the Bronx. That means people don't see you. It's like there's nothing inside you because you got all poured out.

AMERICO: Stop it, Bea. Don't be cruel.

BEATRIZ: I'm not. I'm telling her we're all she has now.

AMERICO: Leave her alone.

BEATRIZ: *(To* DESTINY*)* Destiny, I have a very special relationship with God. That's why I'm not like those other people. I'd like to teach you to have a special relationship with Him, too. Would you like that?

DESTINY: I already have a special relationship...with my friend.

AMERICO: I'm your friend. Beatriz is your friend.

BEATRIZ: Yes, that's right. I'm your friend. Americo is your friend.

DESTINY: I have another friend.

BEATRIZ: *(Worriedly)* Do you?

DESTINY: Yes. He comes when you're not here.

AMERICO: *(Immediately alert)* Who comes?

DESTINY: The Grinch.

(A beat. Both AMERICO *and* BEATRIZ *stare at* DESTINY*.)*

BEATRIZ: *(Simply)* You're lying.

(A beat. DESTINY *says nothing.)*

BEATRIZ: Remember I told you what my grandmother said about lying?

DESTINY: *(Nodding)* Lying is the Devil.

BEATRIZ: That's right. And what happens to you when you lie?

DESTINY: You go to Devil Land.

BEATRIZ: And where is Devil Land?

DESTINY: Devil Land is under the subways.

BEATRIZ: And do you want to go under the subways?

DESTINY: No. I want to go to Puerto Rico with my mommy. I want to be with the Taino Indians.

AMERICO: We're not talking about Puerto Rico now.

BEATRIZ: And I don't want to hear anymore about Tainos.

DESTINY: It's too hot—

BEATRIZ: It's supposed to be hot. It's a boiler room…! You see? *(Pointing towards it)* This is the boiler. It keeps all the apartments in the building nice and warm in the winter.

DESTINY: It's not nice. The boiler's not nice.

BEATRIZ: The boiler is very nice.

DESTINY: No, it's not.

BEATRIZ: Yes, it is.

DESTINY: *(Fiercely)* The boiler is the doorway to Devil Land.

BEATRIZ: Be quiet. Eat your soup. EAT YOUR SOUP!

DESTINY: That's what the Grinch said.

BEATRIZ: I don't want to hear anymore about the Grinch!

AMERICO: Bea—come on, take it easy.

DESTINY: The Grinch said Devil Land isn't under the subways, it's right here, inside the boiler.

(A horrible sound from the boiler. This startles all three of them. BEATRIZ turns angrily towards AMERICO.)

BEATRIZ: I told you to fix that damn thing.

AMERICO: I did fix it.

BEATRIZ: Then why is it making that noise?

AMERICO: I don't know.

DESTINY: It's the Grinch.

BEATRIZ: *(To her)* The Grinch isn't real. There's no such thing...!

AMERICO: Bea—enough!

BEATRIZ: Something that's not real is not good.

AMERICO: Bea—stop it. You have to go now. You're scaring her.

BEATRIZ: I'm scaring her? Did you hear what she said? Did you catch what's been coming out of her mouth?

AMERICO: She doesn't know what she's saying!

BEATRIZ: And what happens when she figures it out?

AMERICO: Bea—

BEATRIZ: It'll be too late. Do you understand that? It'll be too late!

AMERICO: I'm going to take you upstairs...

BEATRIZ: I haven't done anything wrong.

AMERICO: *(Soothing)* No. You haven't done anything wrong. It's alright, Bea—she's with us now.

BEATRIZ: Then why are we going upstairs?

AMERICO: I'm taking you upstairs so you can lie down. Everything's alright; you're just tired and hot. It's too hot in here for you. I'll give you a few pills—

BEATRIZ: No. You can't do that. I can't sleep. I can't sleep now...

AMERICO: Bea—it's alright.

BEATRIZ: No...! I'm afraid for her. And so is God. He knows if Destiny enjoys evil, she'll create more evil. And the Devil will have all the fun. And Americo, God can't let the Devil have any fun...!

(AMERICO gathers up the pot of soup and bowls on a tray and hands it to BEATRIZ.)

AMERICO: You're not going to sleep. You're just going to lie down and rest. I promise.

BEATRIZ: Don't lie to me.

AMERICO: I'm not. You're just going to lie down. That's all. And Destiny is going to stay here. She'll still be here when you get back. I promise.

(They exit. A beat. DESTINY *is suddenly alone again in the Boiler Room. She takes out her copy of How The Grinch Stole Christmas and opens the book. A beat. She motions for her imaginary friend to keep quiet. We hear the* NARRATOR'S VOICE.*)*

NARRATOR'S VOICE: *(Off-Stage)*
Destiny had to be cautious
When reading her book in this place
For Beatriz had said the Grinch was the Devil
And this was due to his sullen, green face.
"But please don't be self-conscious," Destiny assured her olive chum,
"I don't think being green means you're bad.
Green is brilliant and sunny, not glum

DESTINY: And Kermit the Frog is green. He even sings about how happy he is to be green. *(Thinks a moment)* No. Wait a minute. That's wrong.

(We hear humming. DESTINY *takes a moment to listen to the humming, and takes it up herself.)*

DESTINY: That's right. Being green is not easy.
Thank you. *(She listens)*
I don't know. I don't know why it's not easy.
He's a frog, right? What other color is he supposed to be?

NARRATOR'S VOICE: And as Destiny pondered various frog shades
She figured the world was like this as well

Everyone was trapped in their various shades, caught
between a heaven and a hell.
Was she now in a place like this?
A dark place caught between one's sorrows and revels?
Were there people who're green? And were some
people simply—the Devil?

(Blackout. Lights back up to the previous scene. AMERICO
enters.)

AMERICO: She really loves you, you know. Beatriz
really loves you. And you upset her.

DESTINY: I'm sorry.

AMERICO: She's not well...I mean, she gets upset
sometimes...in her head. In her head, you know? And
then, it takes her awhile...to come back. She's had to
go to the hospital...a hospital for people who get sick
in their heads...and...she had to be in there for a long
time.

DESTINY: You mean she's crazy?

AMERICO: No! That's not what I mean...why do you
gotta say things like that? I mean, she gets...she just
gets sad sometimes. And...it's hard for her. She still
sees the doctor. And he gave her pills...to help her to
not be so sad. To help her sleep. *(Slight pause)* You need
to show Beatriz some respect.

*(Lights change. They indicate a shift to an alternate
subconscious reality.)*

NARRATOR'S VOICE: *(Off-stage)* And as the odd man
trudged 'round that hot boiler room
With all the windows covered in wood and tin
He wondered how they'd ever get out of the mess they
were now in
And he realized...he was still hungry!
There'd been no soup for him!

He walked over to the icebox
For cold milk and then, a spoon
He'd have some cereal first
Then go up to see the strange lady, very soon.
And as he settled himself
With his bowl of Cap'n Crunch
He let out an unmitigated sigh...
Looked over to where Destiny sat watching him
And asked—

AMERICO: *(Eating)* So, what's the story on this Grinch
guy?

(Lights change back.)

DESTINY: The Grinch is a monster...
A big, green monster
Who lives in a dark cave
Right next to a place called Who Ville.
And everybody there looks exactly the same.
And the cave the Grinch lives in is really dark.
And he lives with his little dog, Max.
And he's really mean to the dog.

AMERICO: Yeah...right...

DESTINY: But he's not mean just to be mean, you know?
He's mean because his shoes are really tight, and his
heart is really, really, really, really, really, really, really,
really small.

AMERICO: Okay, I get it.

DESTINY: It's like the tiniest heart in the whole world.
It's like a peanut heart. That's why he's so mean. He
don't know any better. He's only nice to kids. Like
Cindy Lou Who.

AMERICO: Nobody's heart is like a peanut. You're a big
girl; you shouldn't be reading silly stuff like that. Give
it to me.

DESTINY: But it's mine.

AMERICO: Beatriz don't like you reading it. And I don't like you reading it either.

DESTINY: *(More whine)* But it's mine.

AMERICO: Where's the other book we gave you? The one about Jesus and his apostles?

DESTINY: It don't have any pictures.

AMERICO: So? It's about Jesus...Jesus don't need pictures.

DESTINY: I think Jesus needs pictures.

AMERICO: Are you trying to be funny?

(Sudden sound of a laugh. AMERICO *is immediately startled; looks towards the boiler. He looks back at* DESTINY, *who continues to stand, watching him calmly.)*

AMERICO: Is that you?

DESTINY: What?

AMERICO: Did you laugh?

DESTINY: No.

*(*AMERICO *stares at her for a moment. He looks around again. A beat. He then continues eating cereal; he also begins to read the newspaper left on the table. He is still obviously troubled by the sound he just heard, but trying to be cool about it.* DESTINY *continues watching him, warily.)*

AMERICO: *(While reading)* Nobody tried to come in through one of the windows, right?

DESTINY: There are no windows; they're all covered.

AMERICO: Yeah but somebody can still come through. Somebody can come if they hear voices...if they hear something loud. So you don't make any kind of noise at all, okay? You just be a good girl and keep quiet. Don't make anyone knock on the glass.

DESTINY: The Grinch don't knock on the glass. He comes in through the pipes.

AMERICO: Destiny—

DESTINY: But he stays near
'Cause I'm here.
(A beat) He'll come in here in the mornings
And he'll have his cereal with me.
And his favorite cereal is Count Chocula.
But Beatriz thinks Count Chocula looks like the Devil, too.
So, the Grinch always has another cereal.
He has Cap'n Crunch instead
(A beat)
But I can tell he don't like it.

(A beat. AMERICO is deliberately ignoring her.)

DESTINY: You know how I can tell?

(A beat. Nothing from AMERICO. DESTINY stares him down. Sighing, he stops eating and turns towards DESTINY.A beat)

AMERICO: How can you tell he don't like it?

DESTINY: *(Smugly; a beat)* He don't eat it.

(AMERICO stares blankly at her for a moment, and then goes back to eating his cereal.)

DESTINY: Do you know what he does instead?

AMERICO: *(Rising anger)* I don't care—

DESTINY: *(Dramatic)* The Grinch takes his long, green fingers
With his long, green, pointy fingernails
And he takes each Cap'n Crunch nugget
Right out of the box
And he licks each one of the nuggets just like this…
(Shows him) and then he puts all of them right back inside the box again.

AMERICO: Destiny, I'm eating, all right?

DESTINY: Except for one, tiny nugget
He keeps that one
And he takes the nugget and crunches, and crunches,
and crunches, and crunches, and crunches, and
crunches, and crunches, and crunches, and crunches
it—

AMERICO: That's enough—

DESTINY: And crunches it in his mouth.
And he makes these faces, like this… *(She grimaces like
the Grinch)*
And he says *(In Grinch voice)*, "Oooh, the noise…!
Noise! Noise!
Of this awful nugget in my head.
Where's my milk? Where's my spoon?
And why can't I have Count Chocula, instead?"

*(AMERICO angrily shoves the cereal bowl back onto the table.
He rises and advances towards DESTINY.)*

AMERICO: Give me the damn book.

DESTINY: *(Recoiling)* Noooo!

AMERICO: There is no Grinch, all right? Beatriz is
right… *Eso son cosas del Diablo…!*

DESTINY: Noooo!

AMERICO: *Dame ese libro ahora pronto—*

DESTINY: MOMMY!

AMERICO: No…no…! *Espere un minuto. (Quickly covering
her mouth) Callate… Callate…S ssh…Calmate…*you have
to be quiet…! It's okay…it's okay, now…

*(AMERICO keeps his hand over DESTINY's mouth and
continues whispering for her to keep still until she begins to
quiet down. A beat. There is a tense moment, as AMERICO*

looks down upon DESTINY. *His body language changes, as he begins to gently stroke her hair.)*

AMERICO: Sssh…Sssh…its okay…It's okay…I'm not going to hurt you. *Tu eres mi hija bonita, tu sabes? Mi muchacha pequeña…!*

*(*AMERICO *slowly moves away from* DESTINY, *keeping his eyes upon her the whole time. The* NARRATOR'S VOICE *is heard.)*

NARRATOR'S VOICE: Now Destiny sensed
There was a fresh dread to fight
For the odd man was seeing her
In a far different light
She'd need to be careful
Without becoming upset
She'd have to learn quickly
How to handle this new threat.

(Blackout. We suddenly hear the sounds of a crude sewing machine. Lights up on BEATRIZ *and* DESTINY. BEATRIZ *is at the table, with a basket of clothes near her. She is working on the make-shift sewing machine as well as with a long pair of crochet needles.* DESTINY *is walking back and forth in front of her cot, watching her. We do not see* AMERICO.*)*

BEATRIZ: I'm a poor woman.
I never went to college. But I'm not dumb.
I know what matters most.
People like me speak honest and simple words. Words that our Savior can understand.
You know…Jesus lived among the poor and he spoke as they spoke, "The meek will he guide in judgment: and the meek will he teach his ways."
My grandmother raised me to fear God.
My grandmother was a dressmaker, too, and every day she would ask me, "Beatriz, did you say your prayers today?"

And if I said no, if I ever had the nerve to say no to her,
she'd stick one of her needles in my ear.
She'd stick me until I bled.
She'd stick me until I hemorrhaged a penance for God.
She'd stick me so I could remember.
(A beat) Destiny, are you listening to me?

DESTINY: *(In a pompous tone; bogus Spanish accent)* My
name is not Destiny. I am a Spanish conquistador.

BEATRIZ: What are you doing?

DESTINY: *(Grandly; striking a pose)* I walk like this
because I have a house on my head. I am a Spanish
conquistador; I have come to conquer the Tainos and
take their gold in the name of Eh-Spain.
Geev me all your gold...

BEATRIZ: You're being very silly.

DESTINY: ...Or I keel you in the name of Queen
Eeesabella of Eh-Spain.

BEATRIZ: *(Humoring her)* Oh no! *(A beat; back to her
sewing)*You have a house on your head. What does that
mean?

DESTINY: My big hat...I was talking about my big hat.

BEATRIZ: You're not wearing a hat—

DESTINY: *(Stamps her foot in frustration)* Noooo...When
the Tainos saw the conquistadors for the first time,
when they came to Puerto Rico...they were all wearing
these big, fancy hats and armor, and gloves, and
carrying flags, and trunks, and all this other stuff—

BEATRIZ: *(Not really listening)* Uh-huh...

DESTINY: ...and that was really weird for the Tainos
'cause they'd never seen people like that before. With
clothes on...and luggage. So, when the Tainos saw the
Spaniards wearing those really big hats, they called

them Men with Houses on Their Heads. 'Cause the
Tainos liked being naked.

BEATRIZ: I don't want to hear about naked Tainos
again. You sound stupid when you talk about that.
Why do you talk about these things? Don't you want to
go to Heaven when you die?

DESTINY: Mami says she's a Taina, so when she dies,
she's probably going to Coabey like all the other
Tainos.

BEATRIZ: What's Coabey?

DESTINY: It's the Puerto Rican version of Heaven.

BEATRIZ: No. There is only one version of Heaven. The
one in the Bible.

DESTINY: There's a Taino version, too.

BEATRIZ: No. There isn't.

DESTINY: Do you know how you can tell if a ghost is a
Taino ghost?

BEATRIZ: Destiny—

DESTINY: It don't have a belly button. Taino ghosts
don't have belly buttons. When they die, their insides
all shrivel up and their body cells shoot out and
become stars in the night sky because the God light
inside them is so bright, it can blind you.

BEATRIZ: That sounds horrible.

DESTINY: No. It's beautiful. The God light protected
the Tainos; it told them they were safe even with the
Conquistadors invading them. I had a dream about a
Taino chief who watches over everyone…he watches
over ALL the Taino ancestors in Coabey, and he's
called Chief Guayaba. He sits on his Dujo stool with
his big, black watchdog, Guabiron, and all the Taino
ghosts come and pay their respects to him because he's
the great Taino Chief of Coabey.

BEATRIZ: The best thing that ever happened to the
Tainos was getting subjugated by the Spaniards. It
was the Spaniards that brought some real culture and
religion to the island. The Tainos were completely
useless and lost until the Spaniards came and finally
began to shape them into something authentic. I bet
your mommy never told you that, right?

DESTINY: I don't know what 'subjugated' means.

BEATRIZ: Subjugate. It means to conquer, to dominate,
to take by force. The Tainos needed to be taken, to
be controlled—that's what I'm saying. They were
like children. They needed it for their own good.
Sometimes people don't know what's good for them.
Now, look at your skin—your pink skin, your light
eyes…your beautiful long, straight hair. Where do you
think that came from?

DESTINY: I don't know.

BEATRIZ: You're white. You're Puerto Rican, but you
have white skin. Like a noble, Spanish princess. And
that gives you power. Remember that. In this country,
it gives you power. Your whiteness puts you in society.
I understand what that power is like. I do. People
are always mistaking me for Cuban, and I don't even
bother to correct them. I know better than that.

DESTINY: My Mami said I was dreaming about my
Taino ancestors. She said they're trying to contact me.

BEATRIZ: Well, they're not.

DESTINY: But what if they are? Mami says this means
I'll be a spiritualist when I grow up. Mami says I'm
blessed. So, she took me to Puerto Rico, next to a town
called Toa Baja and I saw Taino Indians there. They
told me all kinds of stories.

BEATRIZ: You saw only beach bums and fools. Look…
Nobody wants to hear your Taino stories. There are no

Indians here, don't you see? We're Americans...maybe you're too young to understand, but we're not Indians, we are American citizens. Look at me. I got a cousin in Iraq, alright? And they don't send Indians to Iraq, they send Americans. We're not Indians; we're Americans. So, stop arguing.

DESTINY: But Guayaba likes to argue. And he always yells at Yaya. Yaya is the great creator spirit of the whole world.

BEATRIZ: That's enough. I have to finish my work

DESTINY: Yaya's still around, you know. She wants to save everyone. But you can't save everyone. Not if you're bad— *(A beat)* Do you have kids?

BEATRIZ: *(After a pause)* I had a baby once. But he died.

DESTINY: How long will you keep me down here?

BEATRIZ: *(A beat)* I don't know.

DESTINY: You lied to me.

BEATRIZ: Destiny, please—

DESTINY: You did! You said you were going to call my mommy so she could come and give me more money to buy a notebook...

BEATRIZ: I was going to. I wanted to.

DESTINY: You know we don't have a phone in our apartment. You said you were going to call my mommy's cell phone. And then she would come and give me money for a new notebook. But you didn't. I thought you were nice.

BEATRIZ: I wanted to be nice. I did. But I wanted you more. I didn't steal you. I saved you. I don't like your mommy. I started thinking about how much happier you might be with us. And I thought if we were a family, a real family—then I would stop hearing my baby cry.

DESTINY: But you said it died. You said it was dead.

BEATRIZ: Don't say "it". Don't say "it"! He's not an
"it". He was a "he", a "he". He was a little boy. A real,
little boy. His name is Christopher. Was Christopher. I
named him after Saint Christopher who carried Jesus
on his shoulders. And Jesus was so heavy because he
carries the weight of the whole world on him.

DESTINY: You said he cries. If he's dead, how can he
cry?

BEATRIZ: *(Defensive)* I hear him, that's how. I hear him.

DESTINY: Where?

BEATRIZ: Just because he's dead, don't mean he's not
here. He's still here. *(A beat)* Dead people can do that.
They hover. They stay close by. They go through walls.
He's just a baby; he doesn't know where else to go.
He doesn't understand that he's not part of this world
anymore. He's not clever, like you. He can't make up
stories. So he stays with me. He'll move through the
kitchen wall and I'll hear him; I'll close a window, and
I'll feel him move through the bathroom wall, then
through the bedroom door until finally, I'll hear him
right inside my chest, crying out for me.

DESTINY: Why don't you have another baby?

BEATRIZ: Because I don't want to! *(A beat)* Sometimes
I think he might be in Devil Land...but when I think
of my baby in Devil Land, I want to dig a hole so deep
into the ground, under the subways, just dig and dig
and dig with my bare hands, right into the soil, and
pull him out, like a root bursting right from the earth...!

DESTINY: Maybe he's not in Devil Land. Maybe he's in
Coabey.

BEATRIZ: No. I never said he was in Devil Land. That's
not what I said. My baby is in Heaven.

DESTINY: Are you sure?

BEATRIZ: What do you mean? He's in Heaven. All good children go to Heaven. And if you prayed, you would understand that. *(A beat)* Come here.

DESTINY: No.

BEATRIZ: Kneel down. Put your hands together like this... *(Shows her)* ...and put your head down. Yes... just like that. *(A beat)* You look beautiful.

DESTINY: What do I do now?

BEATRIZ: Don't you know? Didn't your mommy ever take you to church? At least once?

DESTINY: No.

BEATRIZ: *(Moving closer)* Well, I'm going to change that. I'm going to teach you how to love God—how to fear God.

DESTINY: I don't want to be afraid.

BEATRIZ: I'm going to teach you the way my grandmother taught me.

(BEATRIZ sticks the needle she's been holding into the child's ear. DESTINY screams, but at the same moment, there is either a light flash or a horrible sound from the boiler [or both] Lights change back. There is the unexpected sound of flapping wings. The fading sounds of a cawing crow. A dark shadow darts above BEATRIZ's head. BEATRIZ sees it and quickly jumps up. She pulls away from DESTINY, holding her wrist. She opens her mouth wide, looks up above her head, she tries to speak, but no words come out... Frightened and angry, she can only stare at DESTINY. The NARRATOR'S VOICE is heard.)

NARRATOR'S VOICE: The strange woman tried to catch her breath
For she knew she'd seen a horrible vision
A ghastly image of death

A black bird, a screaming crow,
It was an omen she could not deny
She'd have to do something quickly
Otherwise someone *(Maybe her)* would surely die.

(Blackout. Lights up. We now only see AMERICO *and* BEATRIZ. *We can see that* BEATRIZ *is visibly shaken and highly agitated; she is still holding her wrist, tightly. We do not see* DESTINY.*)*

BEATRIZ: *(Sharply)* I can't be a mother to this girl! There's a whole other world inside her. I can't be a mother to a world I know nothing about. I'm telling you, Americo—I saw it. It was as if I could feel it; its soft feathers, its black wings...

AMERICO: You stabbed yourself by mistake.

BEATRIZ: No, I didn't...! I heard its cries... "Cawww cawww...! Cawww...!" I saw its black eyes blink at me...like it was saying hello... *(Nervous giggle)* "Hello Beatriz...how do you like the look of my wings? Hmm? Mija, I have something to show you...would you like to see what I have special just for you?" "Cawww...! Cawww...!"

AMERICO: Contra mujer, calmate—

BEATRIZ: It bit me. I felt its beak break open my skin... *(Pulling up her shirtsleeve, she shows him her wound)* look at that...! Look at it! Do you think I'd do this to myself?

AMERICO: Mujer...take it easy...none of this is real.

BEATRIZ: My wrist is turning purple. Look at it! What, this don't look real to you?

AMERICO: Do you hear what you're saying? You stabbed yourself by accident. You stabbed yourself with the needle.

BEATRIZ: No, I didn't...!

AMERICO: This is what you wanted, remember? I was up there the whole fucking morning talking to those cops. Letting them think we haven't seen Destiny for weeks that we got no idea where she is…in the meantime, she's down here, chained to the goddamn floor, and you're sticking needles in her ear…! What's wrong with you?

BEATRIZ: I was trying to teach her to love God. The way my grandmother taught me..

AMERICO: What about the cops? What if they come back and search the building…? You know how far behind I am in my work? You said you would make this easy for me, remember?

BEATRIZ: You're getting something out of this, too.

AMERICO: What do you mean?

BEATRIZ: I see how you look at her.

AMERICO: How do I look at her?

BEATRIZ: Like you're going to eat her.

AMERICO: Aw, Jesus Christ…!

BEATRIZ: You look at her like she's a mountain of rice and beans—

AMERICO: Just shut up, alright?

BEATRIZ: …And you want to climb on top and eat your way through to the bottom.

AMERICO: You're sick, you know that?

BEATRIZ: No, you're the sick one! You're the one who looks at her like that.

AMERICO: I'm not looking at her…

BEATRIZ: It's like you're obsessed. That little, round face of hers—you can't keep your eyes away from it—

AMERICO: Shut up!

BEATRIZ: ...And as soon as she's in front of you, I can feel the hot sin shooting off your body like sweaty bullets. It's disgusting...you're disgusting!

AMERICO: Bea—I swear to God...

BEATRIZ: A father is not supposed to look at his daughter like that.

AMERICO: Shut your fucking mouth...!

BEATRIZ: She's not a woman.

AMERICO: She's got tits like a woman.

(A beat)

BEATRIZ: Yes, she has tits like a woman.

AMERICO: *(Upset)* It's not my fault she makes me look at her like that.

BEATRIZ: I know.

AMERICO: I'm a man and if I see tits, I'm going to look. It's a knee-jerk reaction. *(A short beat)* I just wanted her to like me.

BEATRIZ: I know.

AMERICO: This is your fault. You took her.

BEATRIZ: Don't say that.

AMERICO: Why not? What you did was wrong. You took something that didn't belong to you. We took it— both of us. We're thieves.

BEATRIZ: Okay, yes, we're thieves. But two thieves were hung alongside Jesus Christ. One was saved; the other mocked him and went directly to hell.

AMERICO: This doesn't have to be about God...

BEATRIZ: Americo, everything is about God...!

AMERICO: You talk to her again—when she wakes up. You talk to her. And this time, you talk to her like a mother—you talk to her about La Virgen. About being a good Puerto Rican girl.

BEATRIZ: *(Almost to herself)* There are no good girls left. They all died.

AMERICO: Listen to me. You got to meet this problem head-on. You talk to her. And we make her a good girl again. We make her clean—and then, when she's clean...then we can be a family.

BEATRIZ: You don't get "clean". If you're a sinner who's been marked, you can't get CLEAN...!

AMERICO: What the fuck do you mean, 'marked?

BEATRIZ: "O Lord God, to whom vengeance belongs

Lift up thyself, thou judge of earth,

And render a reward to the proud..."

AMERICO: Beatriz, what are you saying?

BEATRIZ: "*O Lord*, how long shall the wicked triumph? How long shall they utter and speak hard things?"

AMERICO: *(In a fury)* You're out of your fucking mind, you know that? We're not going to hurt Destiny. That wasn't the plan. That was *never* the plan—

BEATRIZ: "They break in pieces, these people, *O Lord*, and they afflict thine heritage..."

AMERICO: She's just a kid—

BEATRIZ: She's not a kid; that's your mistake. You look at her, you look into that sweet face and you see this innocent, little girl—But Americo, she's *not*...!

AMERICO: No—

BEATRIZ: God's put her in our path; he's put this tiny mark—

AMERICO: No way...

BEATRIZ: This little spot...this terrible smudge right there before us so we can wipe out her wickedness in His Holy Name.

AMERICO: She's just a little girl.

BEATRIZ: She's a marked sinner.

AMERICO: You can't make me a part of this.

BEATRIZ: You already are.

AMERICO: I'm not going to hurt her.

BEATRIZ: And what if I put my mouth on it?

(A beat. This stops AMERICO. *He stares at* BEATRIZ, *as though he didn't hear her right.)*

AMERICO: What?

BEATRIZ: What if I promise to do it?

AMERICO: You'd do that?

BEATRIZ: You used to like it when I put my mouth on it, remember?

AMERICO: Yeah, but you don't do it anymore.

BEATRIZ: I'll do it. You want me to do it, Americo? Huh? I'll do it.

AMERICO: Before Christopher, you used to do it. You used to do it then. Even though you didn't like it.

BEATRIZ: No, I like it.

AMERICO: You don't even like what it looks like.

BEATRIZ: I don't care what it looks like.

AMERICO: *(Indicating his crotch)* Go ahead. Do it.

BEATRIZ: What?

AMERICO: Do it. Put your mouth on it.

BEATRIZ: *(Reluctant)* Right now? In front of Destiny?

AMERICO: She's asleep. How many pills did you give her?

BEATRIZ: How many did you see me give her yesterday?

AMERICO: You gave her two.

BEATRIZ: I gave her three tonight.

AMERICO: Well, there you go…she's going to be out for awhile, right? She won't know. Come on…

(BEATRIZ *stares at* AMERICO *for a moment. In a reassuring, loving manner, he puts his hand on the back of her neck, caressing her. She leans over and proceeds to unzip his pants. She positions herself and lowers her head. But she quickly snaps back up.)*

BEATRIZ: I can't. This is what whores do. It's the kind of thing Destiny's mother will do. And I'm your wife.

AMERICO: I knew you wouldn't do it.

BEATRIZ: I'll do it, all right?

AMERICO: You won't do it.

BEATRIZ: I'm just not going to do it right now.

AMERICO: You can't do it.

BEATRIZ: Oh, I can do it. I can do it…! I can do it good. I can do it real good.

AMERICO: No, no, no, no…get off me.

BEATRIZ: *(A little frantic)* I just have to prepare myself for it.

AMERICO: *(Angry and frustrated)* You know, you talk so much shit, but you can't do shit. All you do is talk. All you are is TALK.

BEATRIZ: I'm not just talking. I can do it. I don't know why you're so upset. I know I can do it…!

AMERICO: Destiny can do it.

(A beat. This stops BEATRIZ. *She stares at* AMERICO. *He notices she's shocked by what he has said, and this excites him.)*
That's right. She can do it. I pee in here sometimes. I use Destiny's bucket. And she likes to hold it for me while I pee. She holds it in her hand. She can do it.

BEATRIZ: I don't want to hear it.

AMERICO: *(Aroused, taunting her)* She calls it my "squirting gun". Are you going to squirt again, she asks? Okay. Do you want me to hold it? Okay. I'll hold it if you want me to, Papito.

BEATRIZ: No—

AMERICO: Okay. Do you want to squirt it on my legs? Okay. I'll pull my skirt up for you. Okay. I'll let you squirt it on my round, little ass—

BEATRIZ: Shut up.

AMERICO: She asks me where to put it.

BEATRIZ: Shut up.

AMERICO: She asks me what I want her to do with it.

BEATRIZ: You make her do it.

AMERICO: I don't make her do it.

BEATRIZ: Yes. She puts the idea in your head and then you make her do it.

AMERICO: No, I don't do that, mami. She asks me to show it to her.

BEATRIZ: *(Smacking him)* Shut up. Shut up...!

AMERICO: *(Enjoying himself; aroused)* I show it to her. Yeah. I do that. But then, she just did it.

BEATRIZ: *(Jealous rage)* Then I'll cut her nasty, little hands off...!

AMERICO: Yeah?

BEATRIZ: I'll rip her wicked face open and pour in a whole bottle of hydrogen peroxide. No...no...Agua de Florida...! That's right. I'll pour in a whole bottle of Agua de Florida...!

AMERICO: *(Moving against her)* Oh, yeah?

BEATRIZ: I'll stab her six times in the chest with the heel of my shoe.

AMERICO: *(Excited)* I bet that'll hurt, right?

BEATRIZ: It'll hurt 'cause it'll be the highest, pointiest, sharpest heel I can find in my closet. It'll be as sharp as a knife and I'll slice her puny, little face in half with it.

AMERICO: Oh yeah.

(AMERICO begins to vigorously dry hump BEATRIZ.)

BEATRIZ: I won't let her take you from me. She's not gonna take you from me...!

AMERICO: Oh yeah? How you gonna stop her?

BEATRIZ: I'll light a match and scorch her ears until they turn a hot, bloody pink.

AMERICO: Yeah. You'll burn those little ears right off, right mami?

BEATRIZ: I'll break her head open on the stairwell. I will pull out every single, last hair from her dim, little head. She'll pay for being her mother's daughter.

AMERICO: Yeah, she's just like her mother.

BEATRIZ: DAMN her for making us block the light.

AMERICO: DAMN her for making us cover the windows.

BEATRIZ: DAMN her for keeping us down here, in this filthy hole, watching over her.

AMERICO: In the dark.

BEATRIZ: In the heat.

AMERICO: Kiss me…kiss me, Bea—

(He kisses BEATRIZ *passionately. He has her up against the wall and begins to hike up her skirt and open his pants. Outside the street noises are heard and begin to rise in volume in an almost grotesque manner. Horrible sound from the boiler. Lights out on* BEATRIZ *and* AMERICO. *At that moment, there is a spot on a writhing* DESTINY *who is lying upon her cot. Suddenly, she jumps up, awake and alert. She looks up towards the ceiling. We are able to tell that she is hearing her friend, the Grinch. The* NARRATOR'S VOICE *is heard.)*

NARRATOR'S VOICE: So, the two wicked thieves
Made the beast and forgot the child.
They never realized
All this while
That Destiny was being lectured to
While in her fitful bed.
By visions of a stern, and demanding Grinch
Inside her head.
"Those two need to be taught a lesson," he said.
"It's important that this be done.
If not, I can never guarantee
You'll live to see the new day's sun."
Destiny listened, as she had promised.
"What will we do, Mr. Grinch?" she asked.
"Does this mean I'm done for? Are we going to war?"
Throughout the night, the Grinch continued his whispers
And Destiny giggled as she took note of all he surmised
Their coup de grace might just stand a chance, she thought

DESTINY: And boy…they'll be so surprised. Yes, they'll be surprised.

(Lights slowly start to come down on a nervously giggling DESTINY *and we can also hear the sounds of her giggling imaginary companion. Complete blackout)*

END OF ACT ONE

ACT TWO

(A brief montage; we see BEATRIZ *enter the boiler room with a tray of food. As* DESTINY *walks over,* BEATRIZ *serves her the meal. She begins cleaning from the dinette table as she intently watches* DESTINY *eat everything from her plate as well as drink her glass of milk.* BEATRIZ *then takes the glass from her, places it on tray and exits the boiler room.* DESTINY *moves back towards the cot. The* NARRATOR's VOICE *is heard.)*

NARRATOR'S VOICE: Time passed on in the boiler room.
And talk of killing Destiny
Seemed for now, to be averted
Perhaps they'd move to P R after all
And peace might be asserted

*(*AMERICO *enters.)*

NARRATOR'S VOICE: The odd man had proven effective
In changing the strange lady's mind about slaughter
But was this a calm before the storm?
Was there something far worse in store
For their "pretend" daughter?

*(*BEATRIZ *exits.)*

NARRATOR'S VOICE: The odd man was used to
Destiny's cries
And now comfortable with her as a captive
He began to like the frightened question in her eyes
And as a bully, he'd proven adaptive.

Controlling another's skin
Someone's body and soul
Was proving to be a lure
He could not escape
He told himself it was normal
But if truth be told
His heart was taking on
A far darker shape

(Lights up on DESTINY.*)*

DESTINY: I feel sick.

AMERICO: That's because you didn't eat your lunch.

DESTINY: No. I ate it all. Beatriz always watches me. But now I feel sick.

AMERICO: Maybe your friend, the Grinch, will rub your belly for you.

DESTINY: He's mad at you. He says you keep messing with the boiler.

AMERICO: I don't give a shit what he says. I have to fix it. It's my job.

DESTINY: He says you think you're fixing the boiler, but you're just messing with the vent. He says you should turn the vent off and forget about it. And he doesn't like your cursing.

AMERICO: Yeah…well, he can suck my balls.

DESTINY: *(A beat; she looks at the table.)* My book is gone.

(Another beat)

AMERICO: *(A little sheepish)* Yeah. I know.

DESTINY: Last night, Beatriz gave me an extra pill. She always gives me two, but last night, I counted three pills. You always watch me to make sure I drink it down with my glass of milk. And I fell asleep real fast.

And when I woke up today, I wanted to read my book, but I can't find it. I left it here. You took it, didn't you?

AMERICO: No.

DESTINY: You're not supposed to steal things. If you steal and lie you won't deserve the good heat.

AMERICO: Come on...

DESTINY: You won't deserve the Boriken sun.

AMERICO: Destiny—

DESTINY: That's my favorite book.

AMERICO: The Grinch took it.

(This stops her. A beat. DESTINY stares at him.)

DESTINY: What?

AMERICO: Yeah. He knew we didn't like you reading it. He's your friend, right? Well, he didn't want you to get into trouble. He took the book and gave it to me and Beatriz. I don't know what Beatriz did with it. Maybe she hid it somewhere. Or maybe she just threw it away. I don't know.

(A beat)

DESTINY: But why didn't he tell me? He knows it's my favorite book. He knows how much I love it.

AMERICO: He didn't want you to be angry with him. He wants to protect you. He wants to keep you safe. The Grinch loves you, right? He loves you the way I love Beatriz. The way we all love you. *(A beat)* Beatriz isn't happy with you. She still loves you, but she's not happy. You'll need to be careful. You'll have to watch what you say. Don't talk to her about the book. Don't talk about it anymore. You can't love a book. You can't love something that won't talk back to you. That won't touch you. A book doesn't need you. People need you. You're supposed to love people. And the Grinch knows that. *(A beat)* So, you see? There's nothing wrong, nena. There's nothing to get upset about, right? We're still friends, right?

DESTINY: *(Sulky)* Okay.

AMERICO: Oh, come on! That doesn't sound very convincing. You're still my Taina princess, right? We're still going to be Taino Indians together, aren't we? We're still going to Coabey together, yes? Aren't you taking me to Coabey? You promised—

DESTINY: I don't know.

AMERICO: What do you mean, you don't know?

DESTINY: Maybe you didn't take my book, but you still took me.

AMERICO: So?

DESTINY: You stole me. The way the Grinch stole Christmas.

AMERICO: We took you so you could be part of our family. You complete me and Beatriz. It's the three of us against the world now, Destiny—we're like...the three musketeers...!

DESTINY: But if you steal, you can't go to the good side of Coabey.

AMERICO: You're creeping me out again, you know that?

DESTINY: It's important to be on the good side. You don't want to be on the bad side.

AMERICO: Why not? Huh? What's in the bad side?

DESTINY: The bad side of Coabey is ruled by Juracan
And he's the evil God of the winds.
The bad side is where you try to talk
But all the little pebbles

And sea shells rise up in your throat and they choke you.

It means you're a maboya and there's a bad spirit inside you

So none of the other Taino ghosts will talk to you.

Because they're not allowed.

Because they're scared.

(Sounds of a dog growling. This immediately alerts
AMERICO, *who jumps up.)*

AMERICO: What the fuck was that?

DESTINY: *(Simply)* Guabiron.

AMERICO: Who?

(Dog growls. AMERICO *jumps again.)*

DESTINY: Guabiron, the dog.

He leads souls in through the Coabey fog.

The Grinch calls him Max, but he's not really the Grinch's dog

(Again, the sounds of a dog growling. A horrible sound from the boiler.)

AMERICO: What the fuck...?

DESTINY: And that's the Grinch. But he's still in the boiler.

AMERICO: Destiny, this shit isn't funny—

(A darting shadow passes by AMERICO.*)*

AMERICO: *(Beside himself)* What the...! What the fuck was that? Was that it? Destiny, is that it? Is that the dog?

DESTINY: I don't know... He moves so fast, I can't see him. What did you see?

AMERICO: I don't know. I heard panting...the way an animal does... Jesus Christ!

(Dog growls. AMERICO *pulls out a long screwdriver from his tool belt, and turns towards the direction of the dog noises.)*

AMERICO: *(Terrified)* Motherfucker...! I'll cut your damn head off...that's what I'll fucking do...!

DESTINY: *(Excited)* I see him...! I see Guabiron.

AMERICO: Where? Over where?

DESTINY: *(Pointing)* There!
Right over there.
He's looking right at us.
I don't think he'll budge one inch.
He's right next to the boiler now
And behind him, I'm sure, is the Grinch.

AMERICO: Is he drooling?
You know, from his mouth?
Can you see any white, foamy stuff?

DESTINY: *(Nods)* I know when he gets angry; he makes this strange, little cough.

AMERICO: *(Towards where* DESTINY *is pointing; yelling)* Oh yeah? Well, come on then, you shit...I'll cut your fucking head off!

(The snarls of a dog are heard. AMERICO *continues to lunge at the air.)*

DESTINY: He's not going to hurt you. He's just waiting.

AMERICO: Waiting for what?

DESTINY: To take one of us into Coabey. He waits for Guayaba to give the okay. Guayaba waits for Yaya to okay the okay. Yaya is God. So, Guabiron waits for God. He's a dog of God.

AMERICO: *(Nodding)* I've seen the dog before. I've seen it before. I've heard it growling; I've heard it gnash its

teeth at me. I come down every morning, to check on
the boiler.
And I see the figure of a big, black dog waiting for me
I know it's there.
And my head tells me that this thing's a nasty
motherfucker...
It...it scares the shit out of me... But when I finally get
all the way down, all the way down the stairwell...
there's nothing.
There's *nothing* there.
It can't be real.

DESTINY: *(Not without sympathy)* Maybe it means you're
going to Coabey.

AMERICO: *(Frantic)* Maybe I don't want to fucking go,
all right? I'm still a young man, no jodas. I still got shit
to prove in this world. I've tried to make a good life...
I've tried to be good...but I got trapped, you know? It's
not my fault that I'm in the Bronx, and I'm broke, and
I'm Puerto Rican. Jesus, what the fuck you want me to
do, huh?

DESTINY: I'm Puerto Rican. My *mami's* Puerto Rican.

AMERICO: Don't talk about your *mami*.

DESTINY: And we're not trapped.

AMERICO: *(After a pause)* I don't hear it anymore. Is it
still here?

DESTINY: I don't know. Maybe he's just being quiet
now. But if you've seen him already, you'll probably
see him again.

AMERICO: Yeah? Well, the next time he comes, I'll be
ready for him. I'll be ready.

DESTINY: It might not be enough.

AMERICO: *(All bluster)* I'm not going to be scared. You
hear me, Destiny? I don't know how you're doing this,

but you're not going to frighten me. You're not gonna
get to me, nena. I'm not scared.

DESTINY: I am.

NARRATOR'S VOICE: The panic they were feeling
Strained itself across the room
It was a wound in need of healing.
In this stifling, airless tomb.
They weren't alone in their trepidation
Since fear was catching in its depth and spread
The strange woman had a new frustration
Yet another bump to her troubled head.

(Lights up on BEATRIZ. *She's in a state of extreme
agitation.)*

BEATRIZ: Someone's moving the furniture.
I woke up this morning and the bed was on the other
side of the room.
Americo swears he didn't see anything.
He thinks I moved it myself and forgot about it.
But the bed…the bed was on the other side of the
room!
I'm sure of it. It's never faced the window before.
I moved it back right away. I don't want it facing the
window. I don't want to look at the window.
So, I moved the bed back and it took me forever
because it's so heavy…and this morning… It was right
back in front of the window.
Again.
Now it faces the window—again.
But there's more…before I woke up…before the sun
stung my eyes… I…I felt a hand.
Well, I felt…something…pushing down against my
face…trying to cut off my breath.
The weight of it pushing against my mouth and nose…
and whatever it was…

I think it had...fur...yes—
My God...it had fur on it!
I think it was fur because I felt it.
I felt...the hair. There was hair...there was hair...I'm
sure of it.
There was... a lot of hair.
And it scratched against the skin around my mouth.
And it smelled of heat, and sewage, and the hair was
wet. And this...hairy hand...was trying to kill me.
Because I struggled...against the hand...or
whatever...I tried to breathe and I struggled...against
this...weight...and it only pressed down harder...
against my mouth and my nose...and some of its...
hair...got into my mouth...
I choked on it. I began...to choke on it.
(A beat) I started crying against...the wet hand...and I
must have...passed out or something...because when I
woke up again...the hand was gone. So, I reached over
to take my pills.
Well, I took three pills last night and this morning I'd
hoped
To set aside the pills that I would take for today.
But the pills are not there now. I know I didn't
misplace them.
But they're not where I put them.
(Almost a wail) And now I don't have anymore pills!

(We now see that BEATRIZ *has moved into the boiler room
and* DESTINY *has joined her.)*

BEATRIZ: I'm going to bring you more soup.

DESTINY: I'm not hungry.

BEATRIZ: It's raining today. You know what that
means?

DESTINY: God's crying.

BEATRIZ: Yes.

DESTINY: My mommy says that when it rains, it helps the plants grow. And it don't matter if it's raining in the Bronx, or anyplace else. They still grow. They're still green.

BEATRIZ: But the green is strange. You have to be careful with color.

DESTINY: The rain helps it to keep its color.

BEATRIZ: Well, it rained here on my wedding day. That was a bad sign. That meant bad things would happen during my marriage. Some people say its good luck, when it rains on your wedding day, but they don't know...they don't live in the Bronx. It made sense that I was scared.

DESTINY: You were scared of Americo?

BEATRIZ: Yes. I loved Americo. But I was more scared of getting married. Of being married. The dampness from the rain made my wedding veil stick to my skin, and it felt too much like a shroud. It cut off my breath. I thought I'd die while the priest talked about obeying Americo. And the green outside glowed like radiation.

DESTINY: Don't be scared, Beatriz.

BEATRIZ: That's what my grandmother said...On the day I married Americo, she told me to not be scared, that this is what I had to do...on my wedding night, I had to lie very still and pretend that I was a huge white dove flying off to meet with Jesus Christ in the heavens. She said that way I would fall asleep with nice, pure Christian thoughts in my head. She said that's how a woman shows respect for her husband on their wedding night. She said that's what it means to be good. That's what it means to be a virgin.

DESTINY: Did it work?

(A beat)

BEATRIZ: No. I was still scared. It hurt. I never felt light. I felt blood.

DESTINY: I don't think my mommy lies still and pretends that she's a dove.

BEATRIZ: No, I don't think she does, either. *(A beat)* Does she bring a lot of men home?

DESTINY: Yes.

BEATRIZ: That's because she has no respect for anything.

DESTINY: She's young.

BEATRIZ: That's no excuse.

DESTINY: She says she wants to be my friend more than my mommy.

BEATRIZ: Well, she can't do that.

DESTINY: She pretends she's my big sister sometimes. But only when we have company. And not just men—

BEATRIZ: I don't understand.

DESTINY: She says I can help people.

BEATRIZ: But you can't.

DESTINY: Yes, I can. There are people who live in the building, sometimes they come and they visit me, and I try to help them. You know Mister Gonzalez who lives on the fifth floor? His wife got really sick and died last year. He thought she was trying to visit him in a dream, but he couldn't understand what she was saying to him 'cause she died of lung cancer. And every time she tried to talk to him all this black syrup poured out of her mouth.

BEATRIZ: My God…

DESTINY: It was really bad…he missed her so much. But all the black syrup scared him and he couldn't understand her. She sounded like she was under water. He couldn't hear her. So, mommy brought him to see me. I put my hand on Mister Gonzalez's chest, and then I could hear her.

BEATRIZ: No, you didn't, honey...that's blasphemy. You're not God.

DESTINY: I don't have to be.

BEATRIZ: You shouldn't be lying to these people.

DESTINY: But I'm not. It don't always work anyway. Because mommy says I have to grow up first.

BEATRIZ: You are just a little girl.

DESTINY: That's why you're in pain. You miss Christopher. Would you like me to help you?

(A beat)

BEATRIZ: Stop saying that.

DESTINY: You want to talk to Christopher.

BEATRIZ: But I can't.

DESTINY: You said you can hear him in your chest. That's good... *(Reaching out towards her)* If you let me—

BEATRIZ: *(Recoiling)* Don't touch me.

DESTINY: Don't you want to hear him? You said you can hear him crying.

BEATRIZ: That's different. That happens from my memory. I see him in my mind...!

DESTINY: *(Moving towards her again)* I know. I feel your memory.

BEATRIZ: That's impossible.

DESTINY: What do you hear? *(A beat; she has placed her hand lightly on* BEATRIZ's *chest)* Its okay, Beatriz...what do you hear?

BEATRIZ: I can remember...I remember—

(Lights change. The lights indicate a shift to an alternate subconscious reality. DESTINY *has opened her mouth slightly. Sounds of a child's laughter are heard emanating from inside her mouth.* BEATRIZ *is enthralled by the sounds and leans in towards it.)*

BEATRIZ: You broke me. You opened me.

(Child's laughter becomes louder. BEATRIZ *responds.)*

(Towards DESTINY*)* I can hear him. He's in Heaven, isn't he?

DESTINY: Do you really want to know?

BEATRIZ: Yes…please—

DESTINY: Then wait.

*(*DESTINY *opens her mouth again. We begin to hear a child's crying and gurgling. This continues as* BEATRIZ *moves closer to her. She is touched, and deeply moved, almost reaching out towards* DESTINY…*and then suddenly the sounds begin to change…*BEATRIZ *hears flames, she begins to hear the crash of demons, and then, she is hearing her child in Devil Land.* BEATRIZ *is horrified…)*

BEATRIZ: No! Christopher is in Heaven. He's not in Devil Land. That's a lie!!!

*(*BEATRIZ *runs out.)*

NARRATOR'S VOICE: The strange lady knew this could no longer go on…
There was no more need to restrain
Something GHASTLY had made itself known to her
It was cruel and quite grinchy
And like the lady herself
Completely insane
She'd have to convince the odd man
For the sake of their wedlock
Even if she must scream and cry
The situation was in a deadlock

But Destiny
Evil Destiny…
Needed to pay for her wicked lie
That girl had no gravity
And her cruelty must finally be taken in hand
She must never be allowed to lie again about
Christopher
Especially about Christopher being in Devil Land.

(Lights up. AMERICO *is now with* BEATRIZ. *We do not see*
DESTINY.)

AMERICO: Yesterday morning…I saw them. Its old
Mrs Santiago who lives across the street…she told the
cops she remembered seeing Destiny…the day she
disappeared. She told the cops and Destiny's mother
that she saw her with a woman—

BEATRIZ: No one will believe her. She's old and feeble.

AMERICO: You think they give a shit? I saw Destiny's
mother with them. She was crying. She was trying to
make them understand that they haven't done enough.
They haven't searched enough. I heard her. She looked
pale. But she was pretty aggressive with them. She's
not going to give up. She won't let go. They'll have to
come back. There's no question of it. They're going to
search the entire building.

BEATRIZ: It don't matter—

AMERICO: All the apartments. Even here…in the boiler
room. We have to get Destiny out of here. We have to
get out of here.

BEATRIZ: I'm putting boric acid into all the food I'm
giving her.

(A silence. AMERICO *stares at her.)*

I'm not sure if it'll do the job, but I didn't know what
else to use. It's got to be doing something; she's already

told me she has a stomach ache. She's had it for two days now. But it's not working quickly enough...

AMERICO: How long?

BEATRIZ: Two weeks. We talked about this.

AMERICO: Yeah, but it was talk...just TALK! You know...I thought it was...

BEATRIZ: She lies, Americo...! She says her mother brings her people who want to talk to their dead, loved ones. Destiny says she can speak to the dead.

AMERICO: I know—

BEATRIZ: She has no gravity.

AMERICO: I don't give a fuck what she's got or what she don't got...!

BEATRIZ: She's only waits now for one final push right out of this world.

AMERICO: Bea, this is not a fucking game!

BEATRIZ: I know that.

AMERICO: We have to get out of here. That's it. We pack up and we get out of here.

BEATRIZ: You won't make me a coward.

AMERICO: Bea, please—

BEATRIZ: I won't stay quiet as a cup. We can't afford to. Not this time. We talked about it enough.

AMERICO: *Pero mujer*, talking and killing are two different things—they're different!

BEATRIZ: This is not about killing—

AMERICO: Like hell, it's not!

BEATRIZ: No, it's not! This is not about killing. Don't use the word "kill". This will not be a "kill". A "kill" is mindless. A "kill" is a mechanical, heartless action. Like killing a roach. You don't even think about it. It's

just something you do. We're not like that! We're not
heartless, Americo. We're not mindless, cold-blooded
creatures without souls. A "kill" means we see her
as some kind of dumb animal. Something we need to
destroy and control, or maybe we're just hungry and
we want to eat her. This is nothing like that. This has
religion. This is part of something righteous; something
holy...

(AMERICO *smacks her, cutting her off.* BEATRIZ *cries out
and stares at him in shock and anger.*)

BEATRIZ: Why did you do that?

AMERICO: Because I can't listen to you any longer.
Because everything that comes out of your mouth is
disgusting.
Because I'm not under your power anymore.
Not anymore.
I'm a man.
Didn't I fuck you like a man?
That's right; I said I fucked you. And you liked it.
'Cause I'm a man.
And your power's broken. It broke in me.
It broke when you showed how you feel about Destiny.
The spell broke. It's broken.
You're not a queen for God.
You're not righteous. There's nothing regal about you.
You're empty.

BEATRIZ: That's not true—

AMERICO: *(Realization)* Destiny didn't fill you. She
didn't fill you. Christopher didn't fill you. Nothing can
grow inside a body that's just a wasteland.

BEATRIZ: Stop it.

AMERICO: Jesus didn't fill you. La Virgen didn't
fill you. I didn't fill you…! You're an empty liar. A

hypocrite. I can control a liar. I can have power over a hypocrite. I can fuck an empty queen.

BEATRIZ: *(Rising fury)* I'm not empty...!

AMERICO: Destiny says there's a light inside her.

BEATRIZ: Whatever that girl's got inside her, I've got it, too.

AMERICO: She says there's a light—

BEATRIZ: I'm Puerto Rican in the Bronx. Just like her. I eat rice and beans. Just like her. She is not better than me. If there's a light in her, then I've got it, too. If she sees spirits then I should see them, too. I should see them, too! I have more right to see them than she does. I have more right to hear Christopher than she does. I have the right—she doesn't...!

AMERICO: *(A beat)* What has Christopher got to do with this?

BEATRIZ: She says she hears him in Devil Land.

AMERICO: Who says?

BEATRIZ: Destiny. She says she can hear him in Devil Land...

AMERICO: Oh, for fuck's sake—

BEATRIZ: But I know she's lying... she's lying! Do you know how I know? I know because I made sure that Christopher would *never* go to Devil Land...

AMERICO: *(Another beat)* What do you mean you made sure? How did you make sure?

BEATRIZ: I did what I had to do.

AMERICO: Christopher died, it was an accident. He died.

BEATRIZ: I know...it was an accident. A very bad, terrible accident.

AMERICO: He fell out the window.

BEATRIZ: It was an accident.

AMERICO: Beatriz—

BEATRIZ: It was an accident...!

AMERICO: He fell?

BEATRIZ: *(After a beat)* He slipped out of my hands.
That's all. Like a little, wet seal. I couldn't hold on to
him.

AMERICO: Right...that's what you told me...I
remember.

BEATRIZ: *(A beat)* I was standing in front of the window.
I was holding him.
I was standing in front of the window in our bedroom.
I was there, looking out...
And it was raining again. A cold rain. A miserable,
bitter rain.
But Devil Land was quiet. The ground was still.
And I remember, when I stood there holding
Christopher...I remember it didn't make sense...
because even when it doesn't rain...the concrete still
rumbles at you... It will still remind you of all the bad
children beneath the earth, and then I saw...I saw...

AMERICO: What? What did you see?

BEATRIZ: *(Rising emotion as the memory returns)* The
green. I saw the green.
There were a few trees up ahead,
Next to the parking lot behind the building
And there was ice in one of the trees.
The ice looked like rosaries hanging from the tree limbs
And as I looked into the green
I saw faces...all these faces. They were so pitiful and
sad.

(A beat) They were souls, Americo...they were the souls of every sinful child left in Devil Land.

It was a miracle...somehow...their souls had found some way to hover...to float...to climb up through the earth and into the roots and the bark and through all the tiny veins in the leaves, just so they could speak to me...before they had to go back down to their torment.

AMERICO: No, they didn't, Bea...it was a trick of the light. It was the ice; the reflection off the frost on the trees. That's all—

BEATRIZ: The children! They spoke to me through the green, their breath sifted through the ice and formed a mist surrounding all the foliage... they said it was inevitable that Christopher would end up in Devil Land, too. He was too innocent, too pure. Too good. He was so good. He'd be corrupted. He'd get into trouble. He'd die young. It was inevitable. Because we're in the Bronx, because we're Puerto Ricans, because we're poor...and then...I let go—

AMERICO: Oh my God

BEATRIZ: We are the meek, Americo—

AMERICO: I went down
I went down and found his body...
He was so little, Bea.
He was so tiny.
We only had him for a month, that's all.

BEATRIZ: We are NOT empty. We are the meek.

AMERICO: And at first, I put him in one of the trash cans...
I didn't want you to get into trouble.
I wouldn't let nothing happen to you.
I wouldn't let it.
God...he was so little, Bea. Tiny.
Nobody would've found him

At the bottom of the can.

BEATRIZ: I dropped Christopher so I could save him.

AMERICO: But I couldn't do it.

I couldn't put him in a trashcan and leave him there.

He was my son.

BEATRIZ: I dropped him so he could stay innocent and pure. So, he could go straight to Heaven.

AMERICO: I had to call...somebody. Social Services. Your doctor at the hospital.

And then you got sick in your head.

You went back to the hospital. You were sick for such a long time.

You got the pills.

And I loved you...I loved you and I felt so sorry...and I felt sorry because...

You told me...You told me that it was an accident...! An accident!

But you let go. You didn't hold on.

(Silence. BEATRIZ turns to him.)

BEATRIZ: You can take her.

You can hold her throat

While I plunge in the knife.

And we will *still* be forgiven.

(AMERICO's silence buoys up BEATRIZ's resolve. This is it; she might finally have him.)

BEATRIZ: I'll tell the police it was all your idea...to take her, to steal her...I'll tell them you planned the whole thing. I'll tell them how you threatened me, and that you beat me—

AMERICO: *(Grabbing for her)* You filthy bitch...!

BEATRIZ: I will! I'll tell them you make Destiny hold your thing...I'll tell them you put it inside her...And they'll believe me…they'll believe me 'cause I'll start crying and I'll keep crying and Destiny will start crying, too. And all they'll see is two hysterical, crying females and one angry Puerto Rican and who do you think will get it the worst? Who do you think will be in jail for the rest of his life?

(A dramatic pause. We hear the NARRATOR'S VOICE.*)*

NARRATOR'S VOICE: And the odd man and the strange woman
Could only stand there, hating each other
There was simply nothing left to fix or adjust
They were no longer a twosome
Her wickedness was gruesome!
And his weakness overwhelmed her with disgust.

AMERICO: Yeah…yeah…okay…okay… *(Deep breath; resigned)* Okay, we'll do it. I'll do it. We can't wait for the poison to work.

BEATRIZ: Exactly. We can't wait for Mrs. Santiago to talk to the cops. We have to send Destiny away now. We do it now.

NARRATOR'S VOICE: "How can I kill another person?" the odd man thought, "How can I do this without shaking?"
He knew it would take a colossal nerve
Just to keep himself from quaking.
By hook or by crook, he'd have to build up his pluck
And take his unholy chances in the night
By hook or by crook, he'd need some liquid luck…
Enough to endure his degenerate plight.

(Blackout. Lights up. The rainstorm outside continues; we now hear occasional thunder. Amidst all this, we hear the sounds of AMERICO *off-stage; he is laughing and singing a raucous song to himself, overly loud and obviously drunk.* DESTINY *hears him and hides under her cot.* AMERICO

enters; he is carrying a small hatchet and a half empty bottle of Bacardi Rum.)

AMERICO: *(Singing loudly; slurring)* Pop yourself a bottle
Get some tequila from the store…!
If you're gonna drink…DESTINY!!!!

(As he is singing, he looks around the boiler room, waving the hatchet. He doesn't see DESTINY. He continues singing.)

AMERICO: If you're gonna drink
Might as well drink
Till you hit the floor…!
Got so much liquor in me
Don't know if I can take anymore
Gotta drain the lizard fast
Make sure to lock the bathroom door…!
(A beat; a little sing-song-y) Destiny? Where are you hiding? I know you're here, *mijita*…yes, you're here. I can smell you. You smell like baby powder…and vanilla. All I have to do is follow the smell…and the chain. *(He is near the bed; he bends down and takes hold of the chain)* Don't you know that? Don't you know you can't hide from me? You can't hide from me… *(Laughs and puffs out his chest)* ¡Soy el conquistador!

(AMERICO roughly turns over DESTINY's small cot. Dramatic sounds of thunder. DESTINY screams and runs past the table, but the length of chain will only let her go so far and she falls to the ground. She grabs the shackle around her ankle and vainly tries to pull it off. AMERICO sees this and laughs.)

AMERICO: You can't take it off. Only I can do that. I'm the only one with the key.

DESTINY: *(Yell)* MOMMY! MOMMY! MOMMY!

AMERICO: You think anybody will hear you? With this storm? There's nobody listening…your mommy's not listening anymore...she probably already thinks you're gone...

DESTINY: The Grinch is listening.

AMERICO: *(Fiercely)* No, he ain't!!!! He's left you. He's left you all alone. You're alone. No one's coming for you. *(He gets down on the ground, next to her; he grabs the back of her head)* Your neck's so tiny—this'll be quick.

DESTINY: *(Beginning to cry)* Please don't hurt me...don't hurt me...

AMERICO: *(Propping her body up)* Close your eyes. This is going to be quick, *mijita*—I promise. I promise.

DESTINY: Your axe is small.

AMERICO: But I know how to use it. It'll be quick.

DESTINY: How will you do it?

(Something's changed again. AMERICO begins to slowly caress DESTINY's shoulders, her neck, and her face in an intimate manner. DESTINY is frozen with fear.)

AMERICO: *(Almost as a lover)* I'll ask you to close your eyes and bend your head down. I'll take off your top and push your beautiful, long hair out of the way. I'll come up from behind you and put my hand on the small of your back. I feel how thin you are, how helpless and sweet. Then, I'll bring it down fast. And hard. And then it'll be over. Just like that. I know how to use it. I can use it well.

DESTINY: Will it be painful?

AMERICO: Nothing more than a pinch. I promise *nena*. Don't be scared.

DESTINY: *(Almost frozen with fear)* I won't be. I promise.

AMERICO: Stop crying. I don't want to hurt you.

DESTINY: I'm sorry I've been bad.

AMERICO: You haven't.

DESTINY: I didn't mean to be.

AMERICO: I don't think you're bad.

DESTINY: Please don't hurt me.

AMERICO: I'm sorry. None of this is your fault. I know you're a good girl.

DESTINY: Then don't. Please. *(Pointing)* He knows you don't want to hurt me.

AMERICO: *(Stops rubbing against her)* Who knows?

DESTINY: The Grinch. He's watching us.

AMERICO: *(Gentler)* No, *nena*. There's nobody watching. See? There's nobody else here, but you and me.

DESTINY: I miss my mommy. I want my mommy…!

AMERICO: I said…stop crying. Stop it. *(A beat)* I can't do this. Goddamnit…I can't do this. It's okay. It's okay. I can't do this.

NARRATOR'S VOICE: And the odd man knew
That he spoke the truth
For Destiny's eyes had held him fast
He wouldn't destroy her innocent youth
Her sweetness had finally moved him at last.

(A beat. AMERICO moves away from DESTINY. He sets the hatchet down on the table and takes a swig from the bottle of rum.)

AMERICO: I don't know…you can't stay here, but I can't do this…Fuck her.

(A beat. We hear muffled sounds, a little laughter. DESTINY is listening, intently. There is a sudden flash of light, more laughter, and even AMERICO notices it.)

AMERICO: What the hell was that?

DESTINY: *(Listening to the Grinch)* Sssh…

AMERICO: Destiny…what's going on?

DESTINY: The Grinch says he can help you. He wants to help you with Beatriz. She'll be mad at you again. And he says he can help.

AMERICO: How...can he help?

DESTINY: But you'll have to do something first—

AMERICO: What?

(DESTINY *slowly, almost sensually, lifts her chained leg towards* AMERICO. *He stares at her for a moment, then sits down beside her and begins removing the chain.*)

NARRATOR'S VOICE: Destiny now knew her chance had arrived
And it was clear, she wouldn't have to beg
If the odd man truly wanted her help
He'd first have to take the chain off her pretty leg.

(BEATRIZ *enters and sees* AMERICO *removing the chain.*)

BEATRIZ: Americo...?!!

AMERICO: I'm letting her go.

BEATRIZ: NO! You have to do this now—

(AMERICO *angrily pulls out the long screwdriver from his tool belt and brandishes it towards* BEATRIZ.)

AMERICO: *(Fiercely)* Get away from her or I'll break your neck...!

BEATRIZ: How could you take her chain off?

AMERICO: It's over. We're not going to kill her. Destiny is different. Destiny has religion. She called the black dog to come and save her. She put something in the boiler.

BEATRIZ: What are you saying?

DESTINY: I didn't put the Grinch in there.

AMERICO: You can do that, Destiny. You're different.

BEATRIZ: No. She's not special. There's nothing special about her...!

AMERICO: *(To* DESTINY*)* Tu eres una espiritista. You're a spiritualist.

BEATRIZ: *(To* AMERICO*; crossing herself)* Dear God, Americo, please don't say that.

DESTINY: I have to grow up first.

AMERICO: You can save me.

BEATRIZ: Americo...! Only God can save you.

DESTINY: No, I can't. You stole me. It's not nice to steal.

AMERICO: I know...but Destiny, I learned my lesson. Remember the Grinch? He had to learn his lesson, too, right? You can't steal Christmas, right? Because Christmas ain't something you can see or touch, right? It can only be inside you. Remember?

DESTINY: I guess.

AMERICO: If the Tainos give me their blessing then I can be saved, right?

BEATRIZ: Please, Americo, you've got to stop this.

DESTINY: It's not up to me. It's up to Yaya.

AMERICO: You can show me to her. Bring me to her.

DESTINY: You can go yourself. You have the light.

AMERICO: I can't. I don't.

DESTINY: Yes, you do. Close your eyes.

AMERICO: I can't. It hurts my eyes.

DESTINY: But it's supposed to... What do you see?

AMERICO: *(After a beat; his eyes closed)* I see a stone with three points.
There's a man's face on the stone.
He has legs like a frog and he's angry with me.

There are lights circling the top point, and the lights
are exploding.
They've split open.
I can see inside my body now. And there's nothing
there. Nothing. I'm not Taino, I'm not Indian, I'm not
Puerto Rican, I'm not a man, I'm nothing.

DESTINY: But if we were something once…

AMERICO: I'm only blood and air.
And my germs burst out
Like tiny stars bathed in black coffee.

DESTINY: How can we be nothing now?

AMERICO: And when I open my eyes again
I see each star is glowing
Right through my pores, it shoots out, surrounding me
And the light protects me;
It speaks to me and says it will take all the pain away
so I'll be safe—

DESTINY: *(Excited)* That's the God light. The God light
inside you. You see, Americo…? You see? You have
your own. It's alright. Just close your eyes.

BEATRIZ: *(To* DESTINY; *enraged)* You little bitch…!

(BEATRIZ *chases* DESTINY *around the table for a moment.)*

DESTINY: The Grinch says you better not try to hurt me
anymore!

BEATRIZ: I don't care what he says—I don't give a
damn…!

DESTINY: And Americo says you can't hurt me either.

BEATRIZ: You don't speak for my husband. Come
here…!

*(Lights change. The lights indicate a shift to an alternate
subconscious reality.)*

DESTINY: *(To* BEATRIZ*)* We knew you'd be angry.

BEATRIZ: You won't be saved from Devil Land. This time nothing will save you.

DESTINY: The Grinch knew you'd be upset—

BEATRIZ: Stop talking about that!

DESTINY: It's alright. I won't talk. And Americo won't talk. But the Grinch really wants to talk to you…if you'll listen.

(A beat. BEATRIZ stares at DESTINY; she is unsure of what to say next.)

BEATRIZ: I…don't understand.

DESTINY: *(To AMERICO; gently cajoling)* It's okay…You can talk to her now. I think she can listen to you.

BEATRIZ: Americo?

NARRATOR'S VOICE: And now the time was ready
And everything was complete
Thus, the odd man opened his eyes
And offered the strange lady, a seat.
But it was the WAY he did it…
With his long, grinchy fingers
The way he gestured and touched his ear
It made the strange lady
Hold her breath
It made her suddenly overcome with fear.

(AMERICO opens his eyes; we see his body language has completely changed; this is no longer AMERICO. He turns towards BEATRIZ and reaches his hand towards her, his long fingers signaling for her to sit down. DESTINY moves behind AMERICO. Another beat. BEATRIZ warily sits at the table, across from AMERICO.)

AMERICO: *(With a dramatic flourish)* Atonement…that's the word we'll look at first
Since your spirit is so pathetic and sad.

It's possible you might learn something
About yourself
At least, we hope you realize you've been
BAD.

Now don't look so gloomy; don't just sit there and sulk
Like some Whoo-rific monster ready to tear me apart
I do understand that mine may be of only peanut bulk
But hey, at least I still have a heart.

BEATRIZ: *(Watching him in shocked disbelief)* Americo...?

AMERICO: Pity...that's the second word
It's the one I need to remember
Especially when I think of how much I HATE YOU
And how much your limbs I'd like to dismember.
(Indicating DESTINY*)* Did you think you could snatch
The one thing in my life
And take it like some crook in the night?
I may have stolen the Christmas beast
But I gave it back at the new dawn's light.

(As AMERICO *continues,* DESTINY *hurriedly and excitedly
moves around the boiler room, forcefully pulling away the
cardboard and wooden panels from off the windows, the light
from the outside immediately begins to flood into the room.
The room is changing; it's becoming a place of magic and
dark enchantment.* BEATRIZ *is shocked by what she is seeing.
The all-too familiar droning from the boiler starts up again.)*

BEATRIZ: Destiny...what are you doing? The
windows...!

DESTINY: I'm bringing in the light. The God light...!
And the God light is so bright, it can blind you.

BEATRIZ: But they'll see us from the outside—

AMERICO: They see us already...! We're not in secret,
Beatriz.
We've never been lost to their sight

The Tainos have you in their books, my dear girl
They know you're a vicious animal that bites.

BEATRIZ: *(Frightened)* I am not talking about Tainos—
the police…!

AMERICO: You worry too much.
This whole thing's a cinch
They're going to *condemn* you, not arrest you
Now, listen to your dear friend, the Grinch.

BEATRIZ: You're not the Grinch.

AMERICO: When you dropped Christopher
Did he go, splat…?
What was your real motive
Behind an action like that?
Now, it's all very well to say
That God's your reason
But the truth is, what really scares you
Is just…the rainy season.

(AMERICO looks towards DESTINY and the two of them share a cryptic laugh over this.)

BEATRIZ: Don't say that about Christopher.

AMERICO: *(Fake melodramatic tears)* Oooh,
Christopher…! Christopher…!
You poor, little squashed pancake!
Your mommy's a Who-ribble witch
Whose own grinchiness was a bad mistake!
Did Christopher know his mommy's a racist?
Did he know she hates herself, too?
Well, that's what comes from this kind of living, you know
You end up full of all that icky, self-hating goo…!
But I don't have to tell you that, right?
You're not really capable of such scorn…

It's for the best that Christopher ended up in Devil
Land
Truth is he should never have been born.

BEATRIZ: No! Don't say that...!

(BEATRIZ *reaches over and grabs the long screwdriver that*
AMERICO *has thrown unto the table.* AMERICO *makes a grab
for the screwdriver at the same time. Between them, the two
of them briefly struggle with it.*)

AMERICO: You'll answer for that vicious gleam of tooth
Then down a little way...down a little way...!
Your dark, disordered hair...
Your lips parted with a ruthless sound
Your cold, inhuman stare...!
Then down a little way...down a little way...!
Through the trash
Through the heat
Through the dark
Through the glare
Through the scum
Then down a little way...down a little way...!
Again. And then again. And since there's nothing left
for you
Finally...and lastly
It will all end...!

(*The screwdriver is plunged into* AMERICO'*s chest. Both*
BEATRIZ *and* DESTINY *cry out in shock and fear.* AMERICO
slumps to the ground. BEATRIZ *immediately bends down to
embrace him.*)

DESTINY: Mister Grinch...? Mister Grinch!

BEATRIZ: Stop it. He's not the Grinch. He's not your
damn GRINCH! He's my husband. (*A beat*) Americo?
Americo...!

DESTINY: You killed him.

BEATRIZ: No. It was an accident.

(A horrible sound from the boiler. BEATRIZ *is startled, but* DESTINY *jumps up with glee and claps her hands.)*

DESTINY: Did you hear that? That means the Grinch is okay. He's back in the boiler. He's okay. I'm so happy!

BEATRIZ: *(Still to him)* Americo?

DESTINY: *(A beat)* I'm sorry about Americo. But he's going to Coabey now. The good side. That's why Guabiron came before. Americo was scared, but he didn't understand. If Guabiron comes for you, it means you're going to the good side, not the bad side. It means you're saved.

BEATRIZ: I want to be with Americo.

DESTINY: But you can't now. Americo was going to hurt me, but he didn't. That's what saved him. But you still want to hurt me—

BEATRIZ: No! No, I don't…I swear…

DESTINY: Yes, you do.

BEATRIZ: No…you don't understand…! I just want to be with Americo. Please.

DESTINY: But—

BEATRIZ: I won't hurt you, Destiny.

DESTINY: You won't?

BEATRIZ: No. I swear it. I won't hurt you.

(For a moment, it almost looks as though DESTINY *might believe her, but then there is another horrible sound from the boiler. And this sound is very different. Both* DESTINY *and* BEATRIZ *are obviously affected by it.)*

DESTINY: I'm sorry. The Grinch doesn't believe you.

BEATRIZ: Why? Why not? You can leave…the door's not locked…you can go…you can get out of here!

DESTINY: I can't help you.

BEATRIZ: I won't try and stop you, I promise! I just want to be with my husband…! I can't be here without him. I can't be here.

(The same sound again.)

DESTINY: Juracan is coming for you.

(Again, the sound.)

BEATRIZ: Who's Juracan?

DESTINY: *(Starting to leave)* I'm sorry I have to go…I can't be here when Juracan comes for you.

BEATRIZ: Destiny, please…!

(The sudden sound of Taino drums.)

DESTINY: The Tainos are coming…

BEATRIZ: No…

DESTINY: Yes, yes, they come…Can't you hear the grand drumming?

(The drumming sounds continue. The sounds of wind as well.)

BEATRIZ: *(Looking ahead of her; rising fear)* What is it? What is that?
What's coming through that wall?

DESTINY: It's Juracan and the other maboyas.
They're answering your call.
Can't you see them?
Don't you hear?
This is your real family
The one you truly fear.

BEATRIZ: *(She sees them; horrified)* Oh my God—

(BEATRIZ continues to stare transfixed in the direction of the 'Tainos.')

DESTINY: *(She sees them, too)* Look how beautiful they are.

Their bronze skin is so clean and bright
Their eyes are like tiny stars bathed in black coffee.

BEATRIZ: *(Mesmerized)* Yes, yes…! That must be the God light. Is that right?
It's the eyes of all the Tainos, watching me…their eyes…are keeping me in their sight…

NARRATOR'S VOICE: *(Off-stage)*
And as the Grinch continued to listen
He knew it was time to do as he should
Meting out her punishment was only justified, he thought
It was completely warranted, necessary, and good.

(DESTINY *hurriedly exits.* BEATRIZ *tries to go after her, but there is a sudden, horrible sound from the boiler and another flash of greenish-yellow light. The boiler begins to open. The Taino drums intensify. The green light becomes brighter, richer, and more sinister. We see there is a figure inside. We see the figure is moving. Suddenly, a long, greenish-black, hairy arm has thrust itself out of the boiler and reaches out for* BEATRIZ. *Her eyes widen in shock and fear, and she lets out a horrified scream. Blackout)*

END OF PLAY

www.ingramcontent.com/pod-product-compliance
Lightning Source LLC
Chambersburg PA
CBHW052211090426

42741CB00010B/2493